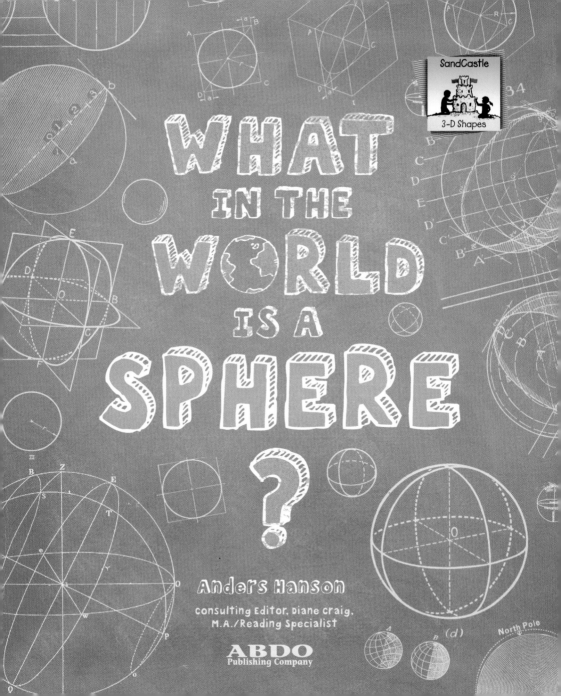

SandCastle
3-D Shapes

WHAT IN THE WORLD IS A SPHERE?

Anders Hanson

consulting Editor, Diane Craig,
M.A./Reading Specialist

ABDO
Publishing Company

Published by ABDO Publishing Company, 8000 West 78th Street, Edina, MN 55439.

Printed in the United States.
Editor: Pam Price
Curriculum Coordinator: Nancy Tuminelly
Cover and Interior Design and Production: Mighty Media
Photo Credits: JupiterImages Corporation, ShutterStock

Library of Congress Cataloging-in-Publication Data

Hanson, Anders, 1980-
  What in the world is a sphere? / Anders Hanson.
      p. cm. -- (3-D shapes)
   ISBN 978-1-59928-891-8
  1. Sphere--Juvenile literature. 2. Shapes--Juvenile literature. 3. Geometry, Solid--Juvenile literature. I. Title.

QA491.H367 2008
516'.156--dc22

                         2007013891

SandCastle™ Level: Transitional

Emerging Readers
(no flags)

Beginning Readers
(1 flag)

Transitional Readers
(2 flags)

Fluent Readers
(3 flags)

SandCastle™ would like to hear from you. Please send us your comments or questions.

sandcastle@abdopublishing.com

SandCastle™ books are created by a team of professional educators, reading specialists, and content developers around five essential components—phonemic awareness, phonics, vocabulary, text comprehension, and fluency—to assist young readers as they develop reading skills and strategies and increase their general knowledge. All books are written, reviewed, and leveled for guided reading, early reading intervention, and Accelerated Reader® programs for use in shared, guided, and independent reading and writing activities to support a balanced approach to literacy instruction. The SandCastle™ series has four levels that correspond to early literacy development. The levels are provided to help teachers and parents select appropriate books for young readers.

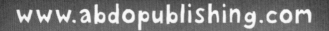
www.abdopublishing.com

3-D shapes are all around us.

3-D stands for 3-dimensional.

It means that an object is not flat.

A sphere is a 3-D shape.

A sphere is a perfectly round ball.

Spheres are completely symmetrical.

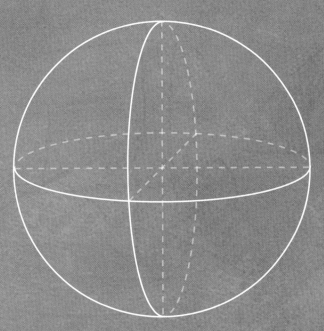

Every point on the surface is the same distance from the center.

Spheres are everywhere!

Jenny plays with
a toy ball.

The ball is a sphere.

Kevin uses a globe
in school.

A globe is a model
of the earth.

A globe is a sphere.

Jim likes to eat tangerines.

A tangerine is shaped like a sphere.

Kelly has fun
blowing bubbles.

Bubbles are
sphere shaped.

Tim likes to play basketball.

Basketballs are spheres.

Derek has a sweet tooth.

He buys gumballs at the candy shop.

Gumballs are spheres.

The earth and the moon are spheres.

Find the sphere!

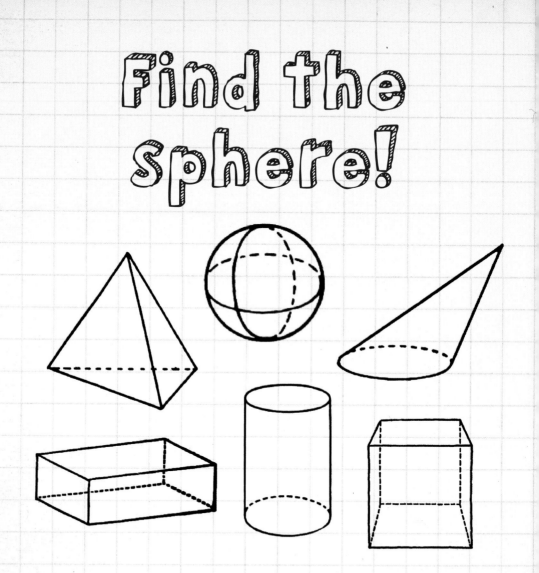

Which of these 3-D shapes is a sphere?

How many spheres can you find in this image?

Everyday spheres

Take a look around you.
Do you see any spheres?

How to draw a sphere

1. **Draw a circle.**

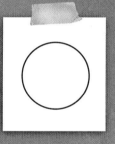

2. **Draw a curve inside the circle.**

3. **Draw another curve going from top to bottom.**

Glossary

dimensional – having a measurement of length, width, or thickness.

everyday – ordinary or usual.

image – a drawing or picture.

surface – the outside layer of something. In geometry, a surface is a shape with length and width but not thickness.

sweet tooth – a desire to eat sweet foods.

symmetrical – having parts on each side of a centerline that are mirror images of each other.

To see a complete list of SandCastle™ books and other nonfiction titles from ABDO Publishing Company, visit www.abdopublishing.com.
8000 West 78th Street, Edina, MN 55439 · 800-800-1312 · 952-831-1632 fax